The Book for My Brother

Tomaž Šalamun

The Book
for My Brother

A HARVEST ORIGINAL
HARCOURT, INC.
Orlando ★ Austin ★ New York ★ San Diego ★ Toronto ★ London

Requests for permission to make copies of any part of the work should be mailed to the following address: Permissions Department, Harcourt, Inc., 6277 Sea Harbor Drive, Orlando, Florida 32887-6777.

www.HarcourtBooks.com

Library of Congress Cataloging-in-Publication Data
Šalamun, Tomaž.
[Knjiga za mojega brata. English]
The book for my brother/Tomaž Šalamun.
p. cm.
I. Title.
PG1919.29.A5K6513 2006
891.8'415—dc22   2005031614
ISBN-13: 978-0-15-603205-6   ISBN-10: 0-15-603205-8

Text set in Dante MT
Designed by April Ward

Printed in the United States of America

First edition

To Andraž Šalamun

*Special thanks to Charlie Simic,
who helped me to edit this book.*

CONTENTS

To Have a Friend *1*

To the Heart *2*

Young Cops *4*

Good Morning *5*

The Apple *7*

Nile *9*

(One day) *10*

History Always Exploits Only Steam *11*

his favorite ride *12*

Incredulous Grandson *14*

1962–1995 *15*

We Club Stars *16*

Look, Brother *17*

threw myself on the lid *19*

The Writing *21*

the lime in the desert *22*

Coming Back *24*

Ballad for Metka Krašovec *25*

Where Are You *29*

Home *30*

Dog *31*

At Night Rabbits 32

Borromini 33

Sheets and Embalming 35

(it's you) 37

Children's Froth, Children's Clothing 38

Cetinje 39

Ring the Bell 40

To Immerse the Weight 41

To Metka 42

Little Fears 43

The Whole of Life 46

Greek Island 48

Day 49

Robi 51

Young Creatures 56

in winter 57

Porcini 58

Kashogi 59

Ridges of aromatic 61

Sonnet of a Slovenian 62

The Flashlight 63

Buffalo 64

It Is Too Hot *66*

(Watching all these) *67*

(Not the murder) *68*

Jumping on the Cart Full of Cantaloupes *69*

Questions for Little Frogs *71*

Snow Is All That's Left *73*

Firmament Above the Cathedral *74*

The Talk with the Hairdresser from Tashkent *75*

Volga *76*

Poem for Cindy Kleine *77*

The Letter *80*

The Circle and the Circle's Argument *82*

Central Park *87*

The Breeding of Prince *89*

Fou de Vincent *91*

again the roads are silent *93*

The Book for My Brother

TO HAVE A FRIEND

I see the devil's head, people, I see his whole body
I never thought he could come so close
he longs for innocence, as we do, I have the sensation
he was crammed into the wall for a long time

I have the feeling that his hands ache, that he is tender
and absorbed in thoughts, he licks everything before killing it,
he bursts into tears, scraping meat, he is blessed
he has no friends, he is walking alone in the world

I have the feeling he is saying something to me
that he is watching me with regret
he knows I could never sleep with him
we are both humiliated

he reminds me of the English teacher
when he was pensioned off, and young secret-police recruits,
it seems his beatitude is failing
the souls squeal when he tortures them

he doesn't drink them, as I imagined
it seems he derives no benefit from them
I think he would like to have a friend
to share goods and pleasure

he steps in the river and wets his head in it
he doesn't know how to speak with it
he splashes on the surface
I will leave him as he is, I will not talk to him

TO THE HEART

Raucous black sky, why did you swallow
my proof?
Who authorized this gluttony?
My brothers are flowers.
Can you still smell haystacks and lemon blossoms?
The body, dipped in water, loses its scent.
The Allahs on the beach smoke their pipes.
All of us burn our eyelashes.
Raucous black sky, did you tally the food?
What will you do in this crowd of white cherries?
Is there a piton in your gluttonous cave?
What kind of papers do you burn under the pagoda?
Don't birds crash into your eyebrows?
You, who can't tell the yolk from the white,
where do you put the colors?
Do you think I'll feed you like an hourglass
which can be turned upside down, into eternity?
I'll break the horseshoe, we'll see if you
keep breathing!
Your gates will burn down
below water level.
Raucous black sky, my intimate!
Display the stones.
Crush the eyes of the otters
so you can smell and count them better.
You're a belt!
No-father!
Your procession of clay and silk flags
goes mad when they touch one another.
Where then is your papier-mâché?
Do the stars wound themselves in my body?

Have you ever asked them a question?
You keep your gods locked up in bowls like peasants
in vats stomping cabbages.
You're deaf!
I've bitten your heel five times already.
And it grows back like the beards of saints,
because they never eat.
The earth is my bonbon, my glutton!
The rest of the fruit we'll divide in half.
I'm beating the rug in your mouth, the black one,
to make you cough!
And I'll roll my children into the fishbones, bend them and
glue them so they straighten up and cut your
throat when you click your tongue and
dream of warmth, because you drank my blood.
Raucous black sky, give me back my number!
Do you see those moist curled paws?
They're yours if you agree to the rules of the game.
Melancholy should flow like a river for us both.

YOUNG COPS

All young cops have soft
mild eyes. Their upbringing is lavish.
They walk between blueberries and ferns,
rescuing grannies from rising waters.
With the motion of a hand they ask for
a snack from those plastic bags. They
sit down on tree stumps, looking at valleys
and thinking of their moms. But woe is me
if a young one gets mad. A Scourge
of God rings, with a club that later you can
borrow to blot your bare feet.
Every cop wears a cap, his head murmuring under it.
A sled rushes down a slope in his dreams.
Whomever he kills, he brings spring to,
whomever he touches has a wound inscribed.
I would give my granny and my
grandpa, my mom and my pa, my wife
and my son to a cop to play with.
He would tie up my granny's white hair,
but he'd probably chop up my son
on the stump of a tree. The cop himself would be sad
that his toy was broken. That's the way they are
when smoking pot: melancholy. They take off
their caps and breathe their tears into them.
Actually, they're like camels riding
in the desert, as if it were the wet palm of a hand.

GOOD MORNING

Buck up, guys.
Don't let depression chew us up.
Bob's awake, Maruška and Ana
were near New York yesterday.
It's autumn today, really autumn
a little colder, more compact.
I'll pack all this terrible melancholy
off into the desert;
die there, scum.
Hyemeyohsts Storm, aka Chulk,
an Indian who spent the year
teaching American kids about peace,
has only five books at home:
Blake and some amusing and bloody
pistol-packing Westerns.
He has a beautiful wife, Sandy, who combs
his long tresses and writes peaceful
books like the one called Seven Arrows.
In mannerist beatitude, I took
one hundred and ten books from the University
of Iowa, and suffered again
the childish conceit of thinking myself a doctor
because I'm paid like an academic.
But I'm not one of those stuffed shirts,
let it be noted.
I'm a poet and I have a tender heart.
All hairy and happy if the black clouds go by.
Bob is stuffing himself with
proteins and cooking some kind of breakfast,
but I say that I'm writing. Rivers
sometimes flood and then they are beaten,

as if it's their fault.
Blockheads. Murder is
an ingredient of love. Maruška and Ana,
come quickly! I love the sea
but why do boats move so
slowly. That's the fault of water, air
is my true element. I was shot through
in the air, that's why I fall so quickly.
And that's why all this energy goes through me,
burns me up.
Bob guffaws. Peter leans calmly on Joan
and writes in California. Then, using my
ability to merge with the body and soul of others,
I become Nijinsky, Pontormo,
or Raymond Roussel. Lots of geniuses
killed themselves because light
tore their heads off, but that's unhealthy.
Mercy's talent is to be reborn.
I am agitated and dangerous. I'd like to be
calm and safe. I would like to die
surrounded by people I love.
With my last strength I would reach out and say:
Come to me, death. I have not lived in vain.

THE APPLE

such an Eros? such a home?
it tumbles, reckless, humus of earth
the woods, brilliant steam of night
the smoke, we name the smoke the surface of the sea
who wallows in the vault?
who supports the hunger of the sky?
where will we put earrings, young lieutenants,
weary sailors?
as if the light itself would show us how to pluck an apple
how to smell it, predatory beast
how ink pencils, ice of mirrors
from the hand descend clouds, who seduces fire in the night?
who knows about loam, about weather? who knows how to
   feed the stove?
herd of hungry mercenary minds
pesky habits, lazy muzzles
Thoth's work coupled common flower beds
steam! steam moves souls! textiles!
breaking hiddens slide
monkeys are hungry, runners are hungry
gifts lick straps, the principle trembles
lying down, I will rake fishes, dry color of crumbs
fencers, baroque stuntmen, huts of mouth
look at loosened world bonds, drunken crickets
buckskin pokes, terrible children
there is bustle in the orbits, rot in mobile fish
breakneck in the heights of eagles

wrappers, rivers of angels, raspberries pierced
on earth we do not file flames, we do not foresee God's temples
we do not turn up our palms
on earth we tremble, destroy waters, nourish smoke
in the dark we lay hands on the hunger of the sun

NILE

The Nile is made of red and black iron. The faces
of the Nile are as smooth as a water smooth plain
and as steep as a hill. The Nile is cut from the
sea by Helwan, from Helwan by El Minya, from El
Minya by El Karnak, from El Karnak by Daka, from
Daka by Wad Medani, from Wad Medani by
Malakal. It is as polished as the body of
a plane. When they carry it away on trucks the grass
is lighter. The Nile is water. Sand rolls along
the bottom. It flows day and night at six miles
per hour. When it reaches the Delta it forms
many branches and all of them flow to the sea.
The surfaces of the planes are smoothly finished.
The height is the same. The first time I saw it
I stood looking at it for a long time.
The police force were lying in the bush. They wore
green uniforms and green ribbon around their hips.

(ONE DAY)

One day in the dining room I measured the exact
distance from the lower left-hand corner of the picture to the
    floor
and the distance from the lower right-hand corner to the floor
as I had the persistent feeling that the picture was slanting
one day I made a bet that dolphins have roe
one day I took the suspenders out of the closet
one day it said in the papers
the King of Cambodia would return our visit
one day I thought who'll be the first one to count up to a
    million
one day I went out in the street to get some exercise
I walked on the right-hand side of the sidewalk
one day it occurred to me that every human being has to die
one day Mr. France bought a grove of birch trees
from a young artist because it occurred to him
that you have to take risks to make money
one day I bought pretzels although that is something I never do
because the dust lies on the street
one day St. Arnolfina appeared on the calendar

HISTORY ALWAYS EXPLOITS ONLY STEAM

Those pits in shit behind the bushes after first rain.
Where did they go?
Don't children steal fruit anymore?
Who still waves the whip in front
of the eyes of cows?
I've heard you'd eat a headboard.
Do it.
The tusk is swinging.
Nero's been hit.
Galician woods are covered in moss.
I catch a doe in the air.
I dilate its legs in the air.
Small hooves, just a little bit with my right and left hands
as in "Buddha caresses pagoda."
Buddha also rows.
You use the throat.
Black honey which is not bitumen.

HIS FAVORITE RIDE

what is your favorite ride
to ride on a steamboat
why
you can see all around
what do you see
the sea
what else
the sky
are you ever afraid of storms
no the boat stays in the harbor if there's a storm
what if a storm comes while you're at sea
then I'm afraid
you can't swim
why are you afraid then
I'm afraid of getting water in my mouth
what animals do you like best
puppydogs
what about lions
I don't like lions
why not
because puppies are scared of them
what do you like most of all
the "Catalog" magazine
what's happening with it now
it fell apart sadly
how come
people don't like us
how come they don't like you
because Marko wrote "the prick's head"
and what did you write
"kitten fucks"

why are you so mean
because we're so sad
didn't you once say you were cheerful
and glad to be alive
I did say I was cheerful and glad to be alive
but as it turns out I'm sad really
what are you up to now
we're going to have a revolution
are you white
no black
when do you feel best
when I'm naked
why
because I feel free then
why do you feel free then
because I'm naked
Tomaž Šalamun is naked and a proletarian

INCREDULOUS GRANDSON

"Children, on the train between Trieste and
  Vienna go to sleep. There's nothing there."
  (my grandmother Mila Gulič, 1891–1978)

Do not nod off
on the train from Venice
to Vienna, my dear
reader.
Slovenia is so
tiny you can easily
miss it! Tinier than my
ranch east of
Sierra!
Better get up,
lean out the window, though it's written:
FORBIDDEN!
Prick up your ears
to my golden voice!

1962–1995

In Dalmatia you didn't sleep at all.
You faked sleep in your sleeping bag.
You kicked my glasses on the cellist
playing at Duke's Palace. We fought about Dostoyevsky
and didn't talk. *Il m'a volé ma voix,*
he said to Madame Bruneau. I complained to her
immediately. I'm depressed. After three hours
the room was alive. I walk because the city
is on strike. I take in Cézanne and step on people's feet.
I write. Andro is in room 8222. But he doesn't call
back. He's shy, he's afraid of me. In Rab we slept
outside. Blessed times when one could still
masturbate in front of the altars. This is what I did
when he went away. He was born the handsome brother.

WE CLUB STARS

We club stars
down from their stems,
apply polish

to our shoes.
We turn around
and sleep

in the same
bed. Do not
be afraid.

This is you.
This is one part
of the same picture.

LOOK, BROTHER

I am abandoning iconoclastic levels, I am a tiger
in a heart a seed bud, the soul germinated in you, did she?
anima, brown sun of unterrestrial strata of roofs
immersed shadows, sheep squeezed in shelter
within palms, dramas
within reach of flock smell, among the petty lumber tradesmen
o light, asunder,
eat fruit, peel the splendor of goods
the meadows are lacerated, the gazelles faster
morbidity, dark fingers, coffee's beauty
of ruins, femme, moments of gravitation
look, brother, blotting papers, dirty putrid chalets
he walked in the land in the year of joy
coming to water, scooping it from the bottom
yielding to the eldest son, to the ship's designers
yielding to beautiful vistas, to the racism of the dream
burning madness of grass, immanent soldiery
I see Cairo from the sky, I see triangle vomiting
the leader of snakes, Rudolph the Emperor's court
are you happy eating?
do you compare steadiness with the color of jute?
with deer rutting, blacks, olive branches?
a brocade, illuminated manuscripts, rise and fall of the family
little Gypsies sit by
who's paying?
I am emanating, eating corn mush with wooden spoons
ceiling and trunk, kneeling, cementing the walls
we pour seed in front of the TV camera
will you stand up? will you wake up? will you sing hymns?
we were plowing, getting firewood for the summer

no need for peace, no need for suns, no need for sorrow,
the thighs are resting, Gypsy
thighs are tired and tremble
the hot blue blood is cut
even before night, even before raging warlocks

THREW MYSELF ON THE LID

warm expanded boiler, flight of the Caravelle
dust on the footsole, gray-green thread wound around the
    thumb
an amulet, ground-up iron plate, place of birth
relation of forest to white bosoms
trembling, drumming, wheat roaring up
dear guests, the back of a llama
hear the child weeping, the woodcutter playing the fiddle
us throwing the sack around the axle eleven times
ducks resting, Pannonian mud
clock ticking, habitus crumbling
stand still, I shall paint an ephebe
dark blue light for long long nights
bee without fins, weary knights
mulattiera, Caporetto, style
how the soul of the earth jacks off the skeleton key,
    sheep-palms
semantic distinctions, sand, cake out of dough
spills out and flickers, trunk hanging down, rain of flour
a gray villain a thorn in the arch
the wing fell into the fishpond, my brother on his sled
the man broke through the ice, people on skis in the mountains
what kind of headgear? what kind of law my poor starving
    people
dark yellow dust trickling off the palm wound with wire in
    Connecticut
drawing board on wooden legs with nails at the bottom
it leaks, it rolls as written down
does not evaporate, sees no stones
does not tremble as we inject the salt
how pilgrims piss, it puzzled me

how many wagons
look, he is small, dark wings, footprints of humans
jiving with the transcendental, butcher's peas
come, I invite you, get drunk, get the message
a cold movement, firing the rifle at the wall
how was it?
it was beautiful
did you speak to him?
he was grinding stones
the net slipped out of David's hands, I threw myself on the lid
I fell asleep, was painted white
woke up and saw what was going on

THE WRITING

The writing
of poetry is
the most

serious
deed in the
world.

As in
love
everything

comes out.
The words tremble
if they are

right.
As the body
trembles in

love,
the words
tremble on paper.

THE LIME IN THE DESERT

the lime in the desert, the wall raised up five inches
Ljubljana, the castle, the roses of huge brown wood
dolphins, the coal, the tractor in the field, *ce n'est pas la pipe*
filings under glass, garden of flowers
who has plucked out the wing?
who drove into the ground four rectangular horseshoes?
the stagnant water, thirty-two fields
the spotted caramel, barbed wire at the corner
the bells, foot-soldiers' tracks in the flour
the prairie fills me, dance, organizing of meetings
we stayed in the line, he was naturalized Greek
around the world with the elephants, inland with the boxes
the circle and the square on the chalk line
the usurpation, colonizing foreign experience
friend or foe?
over Tisa, the bridge, I walked on the long cubic snake
the robbery, this is what is not
squirting brooks of water from the mouth, hugging the trees
the air and the water, the power and the parquet
they took pictures of us, we rolled
we caused humiliation and respect
we traveled at dawn, descended on fields
we breathed wind, loved polite waiters
smelled the pepper, meat, accompanied young ladies holding
    birdcages
observed the sliding aluminum panels of Asia
the Nile, the dark beard and the elegant figure of King
will you move? can we trust you?
shooting light, changes of carriage ·
the turtle from Brač, without topography we die
Southampton, I was armed with chains

the man with rucksack and bicycle stands there by accident
by chance I dived into the sea
Melville would understand, Russian émigrés
let me be unbound, let the temperature go up
let the pencil on white oil last
let the canvas ascend to heaven
I clench my fists, that it may glitter in the sun

COMING BACK

Ash of the snake of the rose,
idols are snowy messengers.
In the gilt edges they splash like a fly in oil.
While the wound accumulates—it can be birds singing—
spirits wake them, not He who does not lament.

The inner bark, cathedral's eyes.
Zipped-up silk on my little slippers.
Jerusalem itself is advancing.
The ox is not moving into the plow.

What right do you have to inflict wounds on the earth?
The coins are drops of sweat
poured out in silver.
Do you, when the peasant bows
with a sole on the nape of his neck,
greet him with the sign of brotherly kiss?

Who are you, Father, I am the bifurcation of rivers.
The child resisting in the cathedral with his
nib. At Chartres I am the sun.
Engraved, fleshy dent of time.

Scales strained on the stone's mildew,
sweet scent of their flower beds—*fave*—I
wipe the Wailing Wall with
a shield, with a flat surface.

The rain transgresses the borders,
the rain is being generous.
The fluff in the blossom is a little circle, and only
crime's dark hour restores my saltiness.

BALLAD FOR METKA KRAŠOVEC

The last time in my life when I was left
unconscious was January 4 in the evening
in Mexico. Dr. Sava entertained me
with dinner,
Benito Cereno,
with dessert,
with Nolde's youth and the story
of how he became a member of
the Melville Society just before
Borges, when he was selling
grease for Yugoslavia.
Once we published together in Gradina.
Greetings, Niš!
But I couldn't listen, in fact I was constantly
thinking of the letter that arrived that morning
from Metka Krašovec. Tiny blue letter
written with letters same as here.
I crashed under the table.
Next morning I visited her in the hotel.
First, for her, I crushed
Krašovec, a sort of fiancé three times removed.
Immediately he flew back to LA. I don't
like incest. I put the rucksack on my
back, constantly wondering why
I fainted. For weeks I dragged her
on buses and fed her
everything: sacred mushrooms
and moon pyramid. With me one sleeps
on hard floors among
scorpions but also there where one plucks
fruit murmuring, you're the color, you're the color.

One day I
broke: with this boy I have
to go to Guatemala, don't you see he appeared to me as
Christ. We were lying on the sand in the
Caribbean, the two of us and a Portuguese whose name
I forgot. Go, she said. I sense I will be
crushed but then
alloyed with you again in the light. I
was afraid. I didn't go anywhere. I took her to sleep
in the motel which was an assembly plant
of white goods for Rio.
Still, she stared calmly into my eyes.
Better look into heaven, woman,
what are you looking at, I shouted.
Long ago I explained to you,
there is nothing left
here. I shuddered when we reached
the Pacific. Salina Cruz, ventilating fans,
prisoners weaving a net.
Naked I wandered on the sand.
Purple plastic bags, the sky, the body, all
purple. Metka! I said. You cannot
pretend you don't know.
You know! Don't throw yourself in the fire!
Go back to that
Academy. In the end they might reproach me,
that I scraped you out. I have to work,
you'll have to travel by yourself, I told
her when we flew back from
Cancun. Why does religion
lose fragrance and taste!
You're crazy! I howled to Carlos, Enrique, and
Roberto, do you want me to be kidnapped

by this woman and put back among
Slavs? Why do you look so fresh,
she asked me coming back from
Morelia. And I no longer knew
who was the grandma and who was the
wolf. You'll miss committee meetings,
it's time to go back, Metka! And I saw her
to the airport. I feared she would blow it up
with her sobbing.
Good-bye! But in fact for me too
the ground started to sink.
My advice to behave as if I were in
Šiška was in fact false.
It's been a long time since anyone was in Šiška.
I called her.
I'm coming to marry you.
Come, she said calmly.
Through the receiver I sensed her
staring into my eyes.
Very very
tall was the man
who threw for me
tarot cards, an old dame from
Persia read my palms.
They all said the same thing.
And I was happy. A chill swept
over me. And I
knocked on the door of my
neighbor Alejandro Gallegos Duval
to tell him I'm happy and that
a chill
was sweeping over me.
Why do we all live so terribly close to each other!

Junoš and Maja said:
he's not as good-looking as you think, but
strange. He really looks like Metka
Krašovec. I flew to Ljubljana on March 27.
I paid thirty-two marks for a cab.
Metka was sick and pale.
I put the blood back into her. She didn't allow me
to wear his ring, she wants me to wear only
hers.
I watched with interest the ushers and my
best man. I finished the precious drinks of
previous guests. Did you, from my reading,
at least buy a beautiful tent for
Montenegro? On Snow Mountain two does
appeared.
I'm here.
My hands beam.
My destiny is America.

In Saratoga Woods, May 1979

WHERE ARE YOU

where are you, irritated crowd, the trap, the ink?
you bitch, ships loaded with maize, old man in Epidauros
squirting, the lacquer, dark burning casks of the gasoline of the
    Christian world
wet woolen rags over the ears, the drill

where are you, Mary, the thorns, Campo Santo?
white blue suits, pilgrims with light
here is petroleum, triangle, the day,
heavy bell, cement ripped apart

where are you, setting hours, burning suns?
hungry running machines, Satan's tide
the earth rolls, the lingam wrapped in paper
hard precision of meter, bag of bread

where are you, noble children, woods of fire?
frozen straps, swords of pure platinum
throngs, killing of herons on the ice, harbors
soft tar in Buñuel, blunt miters

where are the playgrounds between birch trees, equilibrium
outlines of mescaline, golden green bedrizzled planks
here in the sun, almond, April shines
the tribes are opening the boiling mouths of the Lord

HOME

Knee is water, hip is air.
Sensus communis slept four
centuries in the heart of a wild boar, untouched
by a hunter. Where is my
central sky? Nostrils and the ventricles
are brothers, twins. Everyone: Anaxagora,
Pythagoras, the Talmudists, gathers
inside the leaf of a velvety plant
picked by chance on my way
home. Now I know what I have seen:
I smelled it because I needed the key.
There is no difference between a train speeding
through a tunnel, the Milky Way expanding
silently, and a drop that fell upon
the brown leather in August last year.
The eyes of this dog: *sigillum sigillorum*.
I am every step of man touching
the ground.

DOG

Dog! what do you do with your hair?
You roll in the mud like a pig.
You stand up and spray me.
You blink and yawn.

Dog! who was your mother?
Don't you have brothers and sisters? Did
they all leave you and go to sleep behind
some corner? You're hungry. Lazy and mongrel.

Dog! I have never seen you before.
You run on the street and stop.
You run on the sidewalk,
then on the street.

Stars will fall on your head.
You are strange. Leave the
tin cans alone.
Dog! you are so strange.

AT NIGHT RABBITS

At night rabbits
deliberate whether
to dunk

the fat
mother rabbit and
force out

salt.
They wipe their eyes
as do

some
smaller
toads.

BORROMINI

The curtain evaporates. You dare not burn it.
A veil that floats off leaves the heart empty.
Do you hear the trucks whose tires

squeal like massage tools on CNN?
The heart skips its tambourines blinded like
the bags of glass chewed by those painted on

frescoes. Tomtoms and parades and membranes,
snapping of flags. Is your stomach grumbling?
Is it a sign of virtue? Is Atlantis abating, babbling?

If a twig falls in the mountain air, roots
and legs are fried up, a giant hand lifts the back of
a mountain goat as if it were a kitten, the other hand

folds it and puts it down, as if on a mossy dish.
Glues its ears together with Band-Aids, digs a foundation
for a competition. Discovers Borromini in minerals.

Its domes, its mumblety-peg and crosses
in lime. He lay across the threshold and didn't go
out. Sprained his back. Tempted God.

Stretched his skin on a tetrahedron. Broke him up
with his teeth, crucified him, played with him like a ball
running like deer. The theme was suicide.

Swords hung from the ceiling. And in
the silky sun, which did not veil the cupola,
though it was God's sun, quiet frogs listened to

the flag's light, the pulse of silk in the garden.
They wanted to wet him in the fountains. He saved
all the compasses, talked the cows into knocking down

the fences, mooing sacredly in India and laying
down by St. Ivo della Sapienza. The hills would have
burst. He didn't do it, only rocked and rocked,

murmured and fingered the white walls. Ate
dice with pearls. Wiped the dust away with three
fingers and twirled a pine trunk in the backyard.

SHEETS AND EMBALMING

Why don't you wrap up your brother? Sweet and light
yellow crumbs of *pinza*. Out of shutters is
the sky, pins creak as the green

moves and turns. Hinges (not hinges, there are no
hinges), handle, hook, something L-shaped
turned upside down in the left wall, it's not rusty,

it shines *(mi no vado drento, mi no vado
drento)*, now where did you get off to, if
you were at the shutters' opening? Those high

heels, along the pavement in the early morning, a slight
difference in height, so frequently imitated
in poetry, because then the heart really did

break through and has something to do with Gorjan's
suicide and Jure's visit. You wanted to throw me
out the window. If it hadn't been for *bandaio,*

I might be dead now. If it hadn't been for the philosopher,
who would have caught me had the pavement given way,
I wouldn't have been saved. A mystic always sits

on a cushioned seat. Upholsterers compete
with their patterns at the *foires,* to install
their viewpoint. Full of saws and sawdust and the smell of

glue also in the second and third rooms.
Why is Bernanos stronger than rue
des Rosiers? You are not going to play basketball

on the saltworks. *Da me la Battista, da me
la, passa me la Battista, da me la,*
Besides losing your teeth, your aim was off

Kept on throwing,
but what about the score? Civilization zips past me,
you wear that yellow sweatshirt.

Civilization zips past me, in Formula One
you can't see a body, let alone
a helmet, civilization zips past me,

(can you smell grass?) *e mi come un*
vecio maran, I make people happy,
do you understand, *col mio amor cantante.*

(IT'S YOU)

it's you, the whole, it's you
you hold me so I live
so my sword breaks at a curse, death at hope
I kill beasts so that you blind me
so the light shines in the desert, avalanche in fangs
so the fire shines in the middle of the sea, water in sleep
so the glitter and the abyss appear, the numbers of the
    slaughtered
white steamboats nailed into law
arms set on the shoulders
you are, mother, so the air doesn't break, the soul doesn't
    drown
so I glitter after the plague, upright

CHILDREN'S FROTH, CHILDREN'S CLOTHING

Church crypts and branches are on this side of the ice,
on the other side are brushes made of badger's fur and
ether. (Children's froth, children's clothing.) Ice
as the criterion of classification sits here as the sole

guardian; a rheostat, subject to our gaze,
the weather, subject to the oscillations of the sun. Cities
and villages lean on a unit, Heraclitus leans on the fields
where the influence of *brujos liricos* ends. The silver

bellies of birds amalgamate the entire decimal system,
all attentiveness. A peasant in the service of wheat, the
    inherited
gestures of growth are the membrane dirtying the ice. And yet:
    as a string
of human accumulation before peyote, descriptive geometry

is more precious than prayer, because it doesn't embrace the
    errors
of the organic world. Descriptive geometry only meets with an
    explosion,
hence the dated deaths of the sorcerers' apprentices. Fear
    disappears,
perspicacity becomes a burden. For there is no system

guarding it, hence it becomes dangerous and violent. A warrior
in charge of the maximum units of chance knows only
the law: church crypts and branches are on this side of the ice,
on the other side are brushes made of badger's fur and ether.

CETINJE

You cut roads into me,
you wring out my mountains.
I am Montenegro, Black Mountain.

Yes. I stroll
from the pharmacy to the hotel,
the great-grandmother of your white flesh.

The bus skids, shrieks.
Who will stop the soldiers
of Napoleon?

Are you eating at least?
Look, we're on the billboards!
Do you remember Tahiti?

When the waiter with the white tablecloth
killed flies, listened to the radio and
kept saying: yes, yes,

He took more pleasure
in watching us
gaze at each other

than in bringing our food.
From the cut white macadam
where will you skid?

RING THE BELL

You boil that bit of time in between.
The difference between when you come
and when you say you are coming. No. It's
not that simple. I too am no novice.

The difference between the expected and
the real arrival regardless of what you said.
The Bible cannot be read literally. Layers of
uttered time are taken away. But in those

thin little zones, the new shock of time folds and
rattles. I'm watered by longing, knocking my
head into the wall, on the ground, or I burn, burn,
folded up on the couch. With my body and my

mind I experience the delight of all those tormented
before me, or I lie in bed dismantled.
Saints have always been annihilated in strange ways.
Man has always licked his lips because of God.

TO IMMERSE THE WEIGHT

The hunger of cathedrals, silk, the green silk
of pastures steps over the threshold. I see smoke,
a horn, a white mouth. The compactness of the dead
drinks up the sun, as lapis binds the shadow,

fortified in gold. For an instant in the body
of others, we lean, we burn in the field.
Crumbs drink and become bread,
stigmata find directions. Blackbirds, indifferent,

push aside their prey, for only what is seen
can be decanted. Where then does hunger come from?
The frivolity of mountains, laces, fringes?

And their tremendous power to drink up
the kernel, to turn destiny inside out like a glove
and play with the fingers, to immerse the weight?

TO METKA

If I set fire to the white frame of the house, will the flame burn
brighter than the weight falling off our bodies?
Brighter than the samba? Brighter than my juicy head?
I'm in the snow. You are dancing. Under the gigantic

green trees with your sad juicy eyes.
We're listening to the rhymes and slippers of your paintbrush.
Of meadows in which you see moss and what's under
the mixed moss. A white lynx scratching in a dark green throat.

Does the sky ever stop itself up and rattle? Where do you rest?
In an avalanche or on the earth? I gorge myself here, gorge
    myself,
swelling to keep from being torn apart in the heights

by the clouds, pink, blue, and violet, and the flowers,
like Tiepolo, the air cleansing itself behind him,
before the light floods and crushes us.

LITTLE FEARS

I am afraid we will not understand the
mountains. That their warming will be opaque,
though it will spark in the sun on the

snow. I am afraid that the skiers threading
down their snowballs do not need to know the
earth was created. Not a single hair without

love. Every dust and a millimeter of a nail has
its own love history. Not to mention boxes
lying on their backs, already levelled in the

strewn field where engines slide on black
rubber. Foam hardened in a gush stands up
for safety. Yellow color of farm tractors, you

are just putting on another brush and Russians
and Gypsies, among them the local freaks,
smelling the earth, armored and delicate,

are here as birds and birch trees. Onto
you to be dots on the big German rubbish heap.
Your function is on the lessened storks,

watery fish that clean the mouth of
the rhinoceros and crocodile. I am safe
as long as I do not close my eyes. And then only

change gears as on the Munich
autobahn, in the line which will be synchronized
with destiny. Does language when

it needs oxygen call off
the show? Does it allow us to lead it along like a
fat god's offering? Like a magnifying glass

on a little bag with covered clay, for instance
a juicy butcher's cleaver. I don't know why I am
calling it a butcher's cleaver if it is only the

hand sinking. Maybe there are flower beds in
Iceland. Possibly hot smelly air, if it were hot,
but it isn't, it is five o'clock in the

morning, *Loft leðir Reykjavík airport,* the
line by now long ago rooted out from the tunnels
of conceiving. What gives the dancing to wire?

What is this lust for marching when little stools
open up, and now, rush, know what this means.
Would you like to sit down? Would you like to go

to the garden? Are you testing new leather stools
you have bought on sale? Wherever you swing
your paws are full of honey and ice cream. Will

the fish therefore be jealous? Do you see how in the
cuticle the end of paradise is breaking in again,
also knitted into the tissue of the world but it

utlops off and relpeels (Lord knows what this
means), only if it is disturbed in the brightest gulps.
Language combs a bug. Peeling leaves, giving

drink to the cattle, it goes farther and deeper
than the places where conflicts ignite
and maybe they were only welding headgear one to

another, and the one in Babylon was mottled and fine and
they were just stubborn and they could not take it back
before the snake began to talk, because no one

thought to put a ring in its mouth to bring it
under control. Language is the savior of love, of flowers,
of mankind and the instrument of God himself.

THE WHOLE OF LIFE

The whole of life, expecting to find on a walk through
town, past the house on the corner, a giant waiting
to splash you with a pail of milk thirty times

bigger than normal. Hidden. So you can
get stuck in the liquid and count the strokes
of your crawl. So you'll turn head over heels

two, three times in the juice and swim out later.
Does it come from *trampolino* on the *moletto,* from the desire
to know who can perform the most elegant dive? And why

does it happen again in winter, in New Hampshire, on the path
from the library to my cottage, even if there are no houses
between them? Or if there are, you can't hide behind them.

Cindy? Because I once told her she was pretty?
Prettiest was her video in which the twins ate
each other. The twins were on fire. Philip, enraged,

had been waiting three months for his part. In Volosko,
in the master bedroom, with the shades drawn,
stretched out on the clean sheets with the scent of lavender.

Is it really necessary to rest after lunch? Bamboo
glows. And once again you are let loose in the sea
only after five o'clock in the afternoon to get

some sunlight, like the ticking of the clock. *E magari
se avessi il piu bel cazzo del mondo,* can you justify
meddling in all these impossible things?

What *don't* you sting with? The sun draws
lots with its sculpting. It rubs the open blinds
through the parchment. Where to walk

smoothly? Where to set up the feast for the Chinese?
Some play cards in a café. Some never enter
a café. Some tip their servants, some torture them,

and their dusty fingers prove the *Hausverstand.*
And how to know what is allowed, if they have already
fainted by the time you crawl away in your negligee?

Maybe two nights. Not more. A walk on rustling leaves.
Ils sont très pauvres. There, in the middle of the night,
you can run in a rage over the thorns. We cover

all the ditches with turf. If the eye of the tent pole
is too wide we cool it with our breath. No greasy scrap of
   paper
within a mile of here. And in Haloze

we nurse the children going by. So they won't roll
in the leaves anymore. So they won't swing anymore
in the fields, the hearty peasants, because of the wine flies.

GREEK ISLAND

Little hands. If you slice up a cocktail umbrella
and twirl it around in your fingers, they spit
like little dogs who drank too much water. They shuffle.

Their boats barely avoid the rocks. It wasn't clear
if we were escaping under the sea or mainly
at sea level. We were leaving the island in paradise

as tourists. At the same time I was leaving by plane
and my boat and I didn't have two bodies. I saw it
from above, in the light, at seven or eight in the evening,

in August, and from sea level, which was under
my fingers. Burned by manna, splashed with it. She
was walking nearby, our company, which had

discovered the island, loved it and dispersed.
The children of the *nomenclatura* spurt blood.
Sticks spurt honey. Man cannot not compete

for the princess. That's the beauty of communism,
if the aristocracy gets it into heart. First
the view from the air disappeared,

but not from the sea. As if fog thickened in layers,
as if a brush, to the left of the hydrofoil, drew
brown and greasy walls. The boat sped off,

zigzagging, the menacing layers of flysch
intensified. The boat also turned
into a submarine. I remembered the happy view

from above, our beauty. We were all young and happy.
We joked like lazy, overprotected children, who never read
anything, appreciated only the body, and killed for you.

DAY

Maruška sleeps
incense
the road slopes to the sea
the birds are migrating south because of the snow

good morning, how are you
still sleepy and turning over
I had such an ugly dream, that you were captured
and beaten

spank whoever is afraid of being domesticated
the pink elephant
Anselm Hollo brought the pink elephant

old, the Persian signet ring

in the morning we looked at the sky

shawl

Bob was a mailman

peace

shawl
peace

where are you going, so puffed up, serious day?

shame on you
your wigwam will be pulled down
you forgot the degree of Master of Silence
if you abuse the woodcutters, the house will fall on your hands

the letters in the birch tree's bark
can you throw the keys to me, upstairs?

water spouts from the earth, falls like a snowflake

the ship

the cold

blue sky

little eggs, life comes from

ROBI

Sometimes at night, when everyone is asleep,
I cry, because I know I'll go to hell.
Aunt Lisa won't go, and she's fatter than me.
The pillows are prickly.
I can't sleep, because I think too much.
When I don't cry I switch on the light.
The only way to calm myself is to make
a shadow of a little rabbit on the wall.
I don't have any friends, because when I was three
I fell down the stairs.
They say it shook me so badly
that now I'm falling apart.
They call me Trashcan.
Father works all day.
Mother works at the market.
Lisa cooks and beats me, because she can't find a husband.
Everyone is thin at school.
We go to a school with crumbling walls.
The fence is rusty, and if you grab it
your hands turn brown.
I always wipe my hands on the grass
so the rust doesn't get on my pants.
No one comes to pick me up from school anymore.
When I grow up, I'll be alone.
Aunt Lisa watches every penny like a hawk, it's for her dowry,
    and she
never puts enough food on my plate.
I don't eat anything.
Stars must be really light.
And sparrows aren't as light as I thought,
I weighed them myself.

For their size they weigh the same as me.
I'd lose weight if I could fly.
I know how air scrapes your cheeks if you open the window
in a car. Only my legs are normal.
Now I'm saying what I think.
Whoever doesn't say what he thinks goes to pieces.
Big animals form inside me, their backs
pressing against my belly.
Sometimes I think I'm a box in which there is
another Robi.
And in that Robi is another Robi.
Three of us, each going off in all directions by himself.
One day I'll let them both go.
I'll buy a very thin string and tie them by the legs
so they can graze and go their separate ways.
So I can go about day and night without them, and if
my belly shrinks I'll cut the string and they'll
get lost in the space where they graze.
And they say: if someone really wants to lose weight
they shouldn't eat for a week.
But if I left them outside for a week they could
freeze.
They could get lost.
It's not clear if I would be thinner if they didn't exist.
Not clear at all.
And then I might look like I don't even have any arms.
That's right.
They're my arms and my brothers, I have
one on each arm, and inside me, in my body, they
resemble the wings of a butterfly in a cocoon.
One day they'll leave.
And then my arms will wither.
The old arms I'll cast down to hell, I'll go down

the stairs and burn them.
I don't have any other brothers, because Aldo's blond.
One brother can't be blond and the other dark.
I'd like to go to mass by myself, not together,
Aldo can throw himself against the church door, can
lie there flat as a snowball.
Everyone can lie flat.
If it's crowded in church you can't stand face to face with
God.
But now people bring the kitchen stink to
church.
Even if they wash themselves and dress nicely, it's no use, I
can smell food.
I can smell food during the elevation of the host.
I can smell food during the confession.
They won't let me touch Christ.
Once they let people kiss His
feet, but now they want to draw Him
as if he was a gym teacher, and that's disgusting.
Aunt Lisa is the most disgusting of all, because she's
the fattest, and that's why she can't find a husband.
I'll shake the gates at school.
And when Mother comes home she will no longer have
those dead eyes.
And Father will read to me.
The story of the pea.
Why am I the shortest and the fattest?
Why do rabbits mate too?
Couldn't God at least have let the little rabbits
stay pure, they haven't done anything?
Whatever lives and grows—everything mates and the sin at
the edge of the desert keeps chewing.
Bushes.

Grass.
It even dries up the wells known only
to the Arabs.
People mate and their eyes die out.
A man's soul spills out of him from the day of his birth
like wine from a bottle of a drunkard who can no longer
find his mouth.
I'm so fat because I'm keeping my soul.
I'm keeping it for the three of us.
Robi, Robi, Robi, Trashcan, Blob.
It's better to go to hell with your soul than to
go to heaven, if you have to let go at all.
I'll shake those gates even if my pants
turn brown as shit.
The pillows are prickly.
They have turned off my light.
They say I can't sleep with the light on, but
it's the other way around.
I calm down if the light's on, because I can see my
little rabbit.
If I see my little rabbit I can pray for him.
I can pray for every part of my little rabbit's body—
his ears, his little paws, his gray tummy, his little eyes,
if only he had calm little eyes.
If I pray like this for a while and move my hand very slowly
my hand will turn into a little rabbit.
Sometimes he's completely on the wall and sometimes
completely in my hand.
The pillows are prickly.
The window has to be open, and it also has to be
warm.
You suffocate if the window's closed, but
the air shouldn't circulate much either.

Air that circulates mates.
Everything that mates loses its independence.
Air can be diluted in the same way that old sugar
loses its strength.
The air must always be fresh, but inside the soul, inside.
Air should only circulate inside the soul.
I'll cut holes in myself.
Let a rose grow from my wounds so that my little rabbit
will have company.
And let there be a carpet of clover under the rose,
like the Bay of Ankaran.

YOUNG CREATURES

Like irony, the cotton-wadded festivities
grip harder than anthems, harder
than the claws of cancer, the suffocating laughter
massages the sky. Frail little girls so ravaged sometimes

by an attack of the giggles that like leaping gazelles
they rush off to pee, proof of the terrible pressure
inside the body of a young creature. That's why questions
like, please, tell me what's so funny so I can

laugh, too, are incredibly idiotic.
Madam, your soul stuck out for so long
it faded in the air, whereas it just happened
to the young creatures. With men it pushes out

body hair, which makes you think their soul
is made of parallel wicks or ribbons,
while a woman's soul is round as a head.
These are the forms. A burst of laughter is silk.

IN WINTER

here it smells of the Zodiac, of black meat
books *ab aeterno,* dreams
locomotive smoke cloud of Eastern Europe
flock of birds, shouts of railwaymen

card of Babylon, atlases with silver hoods
terrible apothecary's shop *domini canes*
below underwear, golf and flowers
fur cap, baseball glove, Jefferson

Jesus did the same with his own soul
he collected elderberries, epilepsy, prints
liber adversus omnes haereses I beat my meat
it seems as they sing, they singe their fur

so me, my mother, *der heiliche heiland*
three circles of angels, mythical *schund*
we hoe corn, we sow wheat
in winters, when the waters freeze, we'll cross

PORCINI

How do you germinate the lamb, the plucked-off neck, watered
 by milk?
Slovenians, with my tongue I touched your children's palms
and pressed their brains like muscat wine. I give you

back your home. If I pluck off their arms, they come after
them. The torso is my fountain of delight. I roll up
shirtsleeves: Perceval. White knouts with silky

edges are at your disposal. Christ's heart has to be
massaged. I grabbed it with my fingers.
With the hand which I licked. Will the blossom now be

double, Marko? Can you hear the mushrooms grow? I know
you were rooted out, dethreaded, grabbed and milled.
Your heart's sequins goggled. You were blown up.

Wet and moist, you screamed. Your little teeth
fed you. The blueness scrubbed you as with sand.
You plucked out your hair and put it in the herbarium.

Diphtheria. Music's swarm. A ram's head covered with
zinc. Little bags. Little pouches that you can hide
under your armpit. The yellow beak of the blackbird.

Found as a fossil. To be of use? Did you cut them?
All one hundred and three porcini support you. I'm only
 drawing.
I'm only drawing. The ball which runs on my biceps.

KASHOGI

Every holster meets its own insurance.
Where was he cast, where was he dug up, how
deep? Did he protect and scrub greens?

Every holster meets its own insurance.
Bakers too. The ones who fire off their cards
in their sleep are tender and elastic,

charged like chickens. They were singing
mineral water all night. But not the one with
flags, nor the one dripping drop by drop,

but everything only as preparation
for what will break when the day breaks?
First some kind of milk in the mouth and

in the throat. The strain throws you on an open
field as if the sea of Flemish soldiers would
lift their commander and shout hurrah. All you know

is that you're not allowed to bump into a sandwich.
That you had better buckle up. Take the
umbrella against pollen, who knows?

Enough is enough. Pollination can end up as
packets of heroin in a young Ecuadorian,
sniffed by dogs in Miami, turning him inside

out when they followed their dumplings.
The dog was praised. God doesn't flap with
blinkers. In Africa he also sometimes

peels some dessert. He's like the Soča river's
foam if the raft begins to come apart.
Every holster meets its own insurance.

Little hairs whirl. A camel gasps.
Students are my grapes. I make wine from
them. They nobly sign their names as I

too sign my name under vertebral bloody greasy
white blazes of putrid champion. And
Churchill with a cap lying in state,

beneath the knight of peacock feathers, the lodger with
granite scissors soaked with my Evian
amid water lilies in Alabama's red heart.

RIDGES OF AROMATIC

Ridges of aromatic logic,
circular shriek in a soul of white suns,
you, who have come skittering out of your demolished
homes to drink, what can I say to you?
That it hurts me too,
that it hurts everyone?
That you should do your grazing and then get your sleep?
Should I feed your gullet with the sugary smell
of what is to come,
what has long since become
the luster of a dead parallel surface,
the tightly pressed lips of a demystified past?
History—brutal molasses petrified
in the bluntness above our limbs!
Witness, where should I find them water?
Where should I find the law for this slovenly growth?
Should I continue feeding the children as though
they were lumps of coal for barren flames?
Should I again talk eye to eye in
a gray field that is not mine?
That is no longer ours, squealing shadows
of the unfortunate dead, sprinkled with incense.
I am saying something different.
I feel a slackening in the vertical axis of the earth.
Galactic axis, the one we are used to,
breaks. I don't know any more than I see.
Here I am drawing, here I bow down. Only here
does the sobriety of straightened particles
we are contained in hold true.

SONNET OF A SLOVENIAN

The one-legged man with no eyes and a hurdy-gurdy
is selling lottery tickets. What if I took
the tickets and burned them for the one-legged man
with no eyes and a hurdy-gurdy? Note:
Proust's grave was blown up. While I was
lying in the grass with my girl and night
was coming on. While I was chewing on a horsetail
and far below in the village the first lights were
lit. I haven't seen an eagle for a long time.
For a long time we haven't had a proper plague
to sober us up. Corpses were removed on carts covered
with dirt to ease the stench. I drove the flies away
from him with a whip and smoothed the hay with a rake.
A hungry bush likes pricking the dead grass.

THE FLASHLIGHT

Now I stand between
a pine tree wrapped in a diaper, between
a larch wrapped in a diaper, and between
a fern wrapped in
a miniature diaper. My flashlight
shines because it's night. I cough. My
cough reaches further than
the light of my flashlight. I untie both diapers from the trunk.
At the miniature diaper my eyes start
to hurt.
I would like the wolf to come and tear me
apart. This path was walked by one who
smells. I turn my flashlight on
to see where
I am.
Moss is for resting our hands. On moss we
sleep and keep late hours.
Baby Jesus is surrounded by moss
and paper. Not only would I like the wolf
to tear me apart, I want to live
and from the corner of the room throw
a plum on the pool, which is glass on
paper.
But there are no rivers in the desert!
They will domesticate me the same way.

BUFFALO

Bread, when set on fire, burns quite differently than
   the mouth. Chalk files the sheep's
tongue. A blue flame sucks it. When you stretch your hand and
   push away your elbows, do you look for charm in
the hill? Will you leave your bed? A layer of thin water, under

blood?
   The cross, immense heat, little bones dispersed,
broken.
   They screwed into the palm, drove a nail in
the ankle. For all the living juice caught fire without
   coordinates. Dinosaurs, the bending knee and the mass

was overgrown. Madame Curie
   with her nylon trenchcoat,
in the rain, her bicycle leaning against the hut's
   door. She bakes and stirs something in the beaker.
She loves her husband. The gunpowder
   writes on the outer walls, repeats. The king turns around, gets

dreamy, smacks his lips at the murder, reminding me
   of mankind, now
patching its organs. You're kept alive by
   what you drink from my palm. That
delta of time, your blessed eyes, while swallowing
   saliva with chocolates and porn. While your gills

breathe. It hurts that you destroyed my
   letters. Your harpoon can't be
bent or taken apart. You
   languish. Like a suppressed screwdriver,
circled by a female screw. And if I press you
   here? What do you really

feel except revulsion and nausea? What else?
   Why does my hit give you
space? Why do you, tender and soft, twitch
   before you wipe up and
forget? Why do you clutch at hope?
   You complain, you complain to cheer me up.

Then why do you allow yourself to be seduced?

IT IS TOO HOT

It is too hot. The world has lost its white shine.
The boats will dunk, the birds will burst.
The host in the sky will creak and go away.
The smell of rotten gums will stay. The seals

will be rimmed with yellow. We draw as we
drown. Pounds of gentian remain on our
shoulders. Horns crush our knees. It is hard to kneel.
Gently, gently. Breathe in the corpse and carry it on.

There will be round stones on the bottom of the river.
Will the swallows fly low? Who will cut off our arms?
How will the sun fall? Will it catch on fire? Will

the end of the world be of iron, might, and crackle?
Or will we think that mice run around the corners,
the trains on the tracks, my hand on your white red shirt?

(WATCHING ALL THESE)

Watching all these
young men
rot for

not believing
the soul is immortal
I do not fear.

Fear is
only a quarrel about
property.

Hollow
in the middle
does not exist.

(NOT THE MURDER)

Not the murder,
silence brings one back
to the scene of the crime.

JUMPING ON THE CART FULL OF CANTALOUPES

A hammer falls, I crush it for it plays with
knives between the fingers. Trim my silhouette.
Allow the ink to bump, the swampland

to lick its wounds. Silly, as if I were the first to die.
With me you're original, by yourself you're a fool.
I open and close my fist inside your blunt white crusted

snow. Tempests peeled your skin. White gestated
goose waddling on the deck, does it please you if I
don't pry open your yellow beak? If I hold it in my

warm palm and guard your knocking only a little?
You are silk and yellow and you have warm
teeth. The pious ones who soften you, you

will not remember. Little torch, how should I be
respectful? A fragment, a foamy mother fig, you
squatted in the bush. Alternating. The thorn

and the blossom, the blossom and the thorn.
Fluff, if the blossom goes, bang if the thorn.
The root meanwhile sizzles, sizzles and pulls out the rock.

Every other one sinks. The coach has a sack on the bench,
and even if some oxen, I make the keeper out of a cart.
It rises like chi climbing the belfry. It bumps into

pigeon shit. It bumps into bronze potsherd. He
travels like mole and lightning, bouncing between
shepherd and sheep. He ties the hill with raffia.

Wormwood, you should have massaged yourself by now.
The century is the century of a steamer and my eyelids.
My wings are like wings of Pegasus locksmith. I have

many decks to feast on. Little black hoop on my mind,
I'm cutting it for you. Only Etna's crater remains.
I undress inhabitants and throw sandals in your

mouth. Just cook the leather. And sharpen the point
at half past two in the morning, at half past two
with the chain of hungry ones. *C'est la pleine lune.*

QUESTIONS FOR LITTLE FROGS

1

Bast with a monk's frock cut through.
The grave is too haylike.
Fruits lacerate, they abrade.
We have a loaf of bread and the clog this way,
the crime and the punishment.
Mead and gold dust.
Hung on what?

You're little footpaths and you're good.

2

Yet, perhaps I'm a monkey.
A monkey run down by a chick.

3

The fish on summer's hands did not have any highlights.
Allan Grossman's eye is made of flour and I'll eat it.

Are you composed of little fruit pits?
Are you a tree too, the way we are?

4

Little frogs, *buon appetito,* we're invented.
Russians sit on us while riding camels.
We're in the middle of the earth.
We're shaped like little frogs, the second time,
and when I name them for the third time,
the little frogs, they'll dry up.

5

When God reads brushwood
(little soul, a shovel) he's neither bitten through nor does he
go on with biting through.

You're in the thread, you're not in the non-thread.

6

Your pinch is my rustic Kugel.
Power is the power of reinstatement.

I washed myself, I cut my hair and obeyed, so that
the cannon collapsed.

7

The diatribe dived in the marmot.
I could wash three little flies at once.

8

L'angoisse gives way.
Curiosity below the green paper is paneled.

9

Trees grow into the sky.
I'm glad for the oak and the mousetrap.

SNOW IS ALL THAT'S LEFT

I think about God instead of thinking
of snow. Not true.
God thinks about me and eats me.
No one thinks about anyone.
A little cart goes down the road.
Snow falls when it falls.
God is a perfect stranger, he is not planted by anyone.
I'd like to be planted like a willow.
I'd like to be planted like grass.
And then fall upon it like snow, softly.
We would fall asleep and uncover God's blanket, my
skin, and disappear in the street, into the night.
Yesterday I walked by the swinging doors.
Doors from knees to chest.
I went in to see if the angel was there.
There was an old man with a sombrero.
With dark skin and even darker eyes.
I spilled tequila.
I knocked it back.
The sound was not that of opening
a pipe for water to flow.
I need to drink tequila.
I need to be a tree, planted in the earth, and
push the door.
I need to meet an angel.

FIRMAMENT ABOVE THE CATHEDRAL

Šalamun, Šalamun,
there is none we crushed it.
With his eyes he stared at Brutus.
Six of them became lotuslike.
In the yellow buildings and types of people.
Is it not a giant who hugs the pillars of Chartres?
His palm is between rose window and rose window,
the heather in his palm is soft violet, almost
crimson. One blossom like a bag made of straw.
The enlargement, approximately three hundred
times, as with the senses when the Japanese man
who ate the Parisian lady he kept in the fridge.
Goethe had done this with praying mantises.
Crickets and drawn beetles, they were
phantasmagoric.
He waited. He did not remember
Visočnik. Visočnik with his miner's cap, close to
a seal in the boat. The boat's inner edge
freezes. In the cap, on the sheet metal, with
the glove. With water splashing in boots.
Those who come, not lighting the stoves!
A cherry falls with antiquity.
God did not lick tribes.
The fur cap is made of paper and always
organic hair. As with my mother who thought
my shares were painted. I eat the building.
In the hoop I am the father of meat.

THE TALK WITH THE HAIRDRESSER
FROM TASHKENT

In New York City you have all you truly need.
A Chinese laundry to wash your clothes,
a cinema to watch the monsters and
the vase pushing itself to the sky.

The only important thing is
not to allow my newborn,
splashing and sticking
his little feet out across the edge
of the chalice, to get cold.

VOLGA

In Mandelstam everything comes from the pores and
is fragrant. From the pleasant scent
of bodies in the Volga. There are apples, Mother Nature's gift,

and the teeth crunch them. It hurts precisely when he
minces with Nadezhda, even when he drags
a factory after him. And he throws out

the children of the Nile, he's free of them. He
wraps them in droppings made from butterflies,
illuminating Egypt like sacred beetles. Nadezhda!

Genes will lure us into the swamp. I have them
with the Russian ones. The Russian ones advance
in high boots with their mustaches. Their

legs swim inside two big boutiques. Cossacks
don't know their way around. Lay a stocking
under the boat and coo it out, little dove.

You just don't care for me as much as you did. Only
the conical bamboo can run over the hidden wild boar
with its back wheels. Little snouts, you're in a malt.

POEM FOR CINDY KLEINE

First I sigh.
Gratia.
My lungs expand, become bigger,
a rock coiled with canvas, then velvet.
It boils.
As if the earth is arranging itself.
The heat is on, it babbles, it bursts, it ripples,
my belly rumbles, I type.
Cindy's legs burn, I look with her eyes—
Gus's father's shoulders burn in blue flames.
Gus stares like a dog.
Gus is kind.
He is incredibly kind.
He gave me a gift of raspberries.
Cindy's hair is like a stone sculpture,
Lady of the Flowers, American edition's jacket,
Grove Press.
A thumb is my wounded skier.
Hello, Father!
You are girded.
Cindy puts on lipstick.
I lifted her, she has a thin, thin, delicate body.
I embraced her.
On the rug I showed her how the nuns jumped
on St. John of the Cross, upon his limbs.
She was pale as a small tread, a small tread.
Her twins lick each other.
When they open their mouths, one of their mouths burns.
Her grandmother gives them a jacket.
She pushes it into their hands.
She says, here, take it.

Her grandmother wants to give them a jacket.
The twins divide their woman,
she is the caulking between them.
The woman goes away.
Waves crash upon the coast.
The earth's ribs are pulled up.
It hurts! A turnip! A turnip!
What kind of water will flood these spaces?
I think of friends who live in valleys.
We should all go to the hills, at least
sixty, seventy, eighty meters high.
At least two hundred feet high.
Drive away!
Go away on foot, walk, the flood is coming.
Cindy should go at the very least to a skyscraper in Boston.
O the Charles River!
Her body should bend over the mound.
To be stuck. Not to slip.
At least one third of her body must be caulked
to the other side of the hill.
If you sprinkle her with sand, sand burns.
I turn the corner, a big asparagus stabs
the wall at the height of my eyes. A soft tombstone
with a turban, a gray one, made of wool. It swims in the air,
it still swims, it wants to remain there with its head
stabbing the wall, for a while it swings, then comes
unstuck and falls.
I am at the wheel.
Untouched.
The event has the same meaning as the previous one,
Peterborough, New Hampshire, December 23, 1986,
when a huge tub of milk
(about thirty, forty liters) spilled over me.

From the hand of the housewife, by the instructions of
Father, only that the form of these people is
eight to ten times bigger.
As if man could pour four liters of milk all at once.
And I was sweet and wet
and I knew everything was kind,
although I coughed and barely breathed and watched.
The milk left no trace on the ground.

THE LETTER

Red, burgundy, blue,
this is my roof, I belong here.
Bread crumbs, jugs, paper, and
the wind lifting all of this to sea.
They bump the hull of a steamboat.
O how I call the body of my younger
self, I would like to hug him.
Why are you not here?
What are you afraid of?
We'll slit the spiral if you want,
we'll crucify the document.
Sun on red bricks in the sunset
will be ours, the continent will be ours.
We'll crush our cradle under the belly of a boat
and get up safe, refreshed.
Come!
Look, I splintered all the New York
bridges into pirouettes,
people are choking, hamsters aren't getting water,
and a huge avalanche,
our sea and a great fair,
kingfishers braking
through the austere air, soft and crystal,
through the father of gelatin,
land on our shoulders.

Cabbies are happy.
The world turns up where we rub our sleeves.
We can concentrate the night into a pump and a dumpling.
We dissolve gold.
Something in between wooden tubs and gas cans,
bent blue edge and body made of metal.
We know everything and we know it only here.
Bobby, leave him!

THE CIRCLE AND THE CIRCLE'S ARGUMENT

1
Flower, yellow
flower,
who gave you milk?

2
The night is violet,
thorns are white, blood not blood.
Now it flows toward the sneaker,
the sneaker lies on the ground,
I sit.
Where is the turning point, where is
the law that binds blood, that drips
to blood, that lies on the parquet floor?
Wood, do you feel?

3
I bite you, all of you, dust.

A stone comes flying into the chestnut tree.

These human hands cut the wheat,
caress and beat the cows.

Millions and millions and millions
of rivers for a white circle
no bigger than my finger.

The Alsatian's house collapses.
The bell's skirt curls up.
Red! How?
Are you on the way? Are you on the way
on foot into the eye?
Does the sun send you? Does it
give you a push?

4
I do not forget your name,
windhover.
I do not know you.
Among birds
I would not recognize you.

Nature digs into
my mirror's metal.

Laugh! Through the Thousand and One
Nights I see cabbage.
The cold comes down from the clouds.

5
Mama!
Down there, in the ditch
a man is sleeping on his back.

Strangle God so he can sleep in peace.
Get some rest.

Air enters the skin.
Doesn't stop until it dies.
Air squeezes through.
Doesn't stop until razor
sharp.

6

I am a woman.
With a pencil I draw on thin
sheets of paper.
I pierce the paper's soul.
Only the oak chests I coat with lacquer.

Little ants from my back are now in my fist.
They buzz inside my fist.
Who uprooted them?

The tunnel is a whistle.
Grow, become a giant,
two giants.
Your body will cover the shepherd's soul.

7

Good wishes invent only trains.
Only on the first day does the Lord travel inside them.
Only if the Lord stands up, if he
stretches, if the windows and the metal casing
merge with grass (the unwounded), can memory
persist. Memory is touch. Touch is
eternity.

Geniuses are kilos of pain inside the earth's bosom.
The bosom screams with joy. It clasps. Through it
the real music is heard.

Let us kill the peacock that is not guilty.
To kill the guilty one, the wolf, would mean
to miss a chance.

This is how I see the blossom, to give us resin.
The tree trunks will take revenge on me, all the tree trunks.
Ever since I've been on this earth, they've bled
for nothing.

8
Stop, drop it!
Who gives the seed the right to grow?

I do.
This is why I shiver.

I am an animal.
I lie on my back.
Tongues of flame exit my head.
You should say if I am the sacred cow.
I am mute as a sphere.

Of all things, death is the mildest.
Water captures it.
I am the water.

9
To be God is first class.

Those who don't know me by heart will be erased.

I breathe the same air you breathe.
Green for me is green for you.
My throat constricts.
I don't understand why I was chosen.

Brothers, come help me.
Snails, titmice, crickets, cicadas,
flies, woodpeckers, sparrows.
Come help me, water, which you, blackbird,
carry in your beak.
I saw you when you drank.
I saw you when you drank.
It did not make you burst.
The water made me explode. I exploded.
I am the X ray of the white magnolia.

10
Leave the ladder, you'll never catch up with me.
I would like to give you everything, really everything.
Grease, skin, hair, eyes, tongue,
nails, juice, blood. I would like for us to go
together, I really would.
Believe me.
I do not understand, why me.

Only for Nijinsky was it also this way.
Lion, how are you? They put you in a cage!
The madman's a vapor.
The madman's a vapor.
Kill me, I circle your madness!
I take everything from everyone because I'm God.

To be God is first class.

Do you understand the title now?

It's provisional.
The true one is
MURDER.

CENTRAL PARK

Who eats all the time?
The Kents who killed the Vanderbilts
and zipped up the eyes of crocodiles?

Or agaves glazing their
footstools? The spike hurts. The dew hurts.
That shine Basquiat witnessed upon seeing

Picasso was eaten by his mother. I don't like
hot themes anymore. They blow into the pure
delight and human cloth remains lying.

When shoeing a horse this infliction is even
heavier, you can imagine how it
hurts. Is rawhide ransomed back?

Do they change trains and putrefaction?
If we remodel the cellar, can a Christmas
toy train tear down the wall, can dynamics

and attestations really come back?
Will pastry mature backwards? Will they move,
from the straw to the coat of arms? Let's say

we come to the creature stuffed to resemble a date.
Juice, the sun, and here and there a bit of sand
to remember the dunes between teeth.

Needless to say you stamp it. If Ajax or
Peter, Leda or the swan, stones folded like
hills in Central Park, did the sheep really keep

late hours on this brown lawn? They
pretended to be gold. They whistled with their
sheepskin coats and little thigh pulses.

Butterflies peeled chinchillas. The count, needless to say
came here to escape so you could graze yourself
full. I'm cheating on Kent, not with Isaac.

THE BREEDING OF PRINCE

I

O you, young man, Herostratus,
you burn wood where there are no woods.

Ask the women of this world
how mighty I am, how sweet!
Ask the eyes of my offspring—
tender, gorgeous lakes.
I'm the sun, salty moist king,
my hips are courts
to landscapes and hills.
Ask the women of this world if they
melted under my ease and vigor,
under my club,
under my honey.
If they suffered in azure shade
and fainted from speed,
if I hammered them to the ground
with my flames.
What are you doing
in my life, then, young man,
my lion, my lamb, my prince.
I gave you eyesight.
Your limbs are my limbs.
I gave you blood.
Your blood is my blood.
Why then do you mess with me,
gigolo painter, trying to
escape and revoke
the seal;

star, glittering in my
energy.

II

Peony, who boiled onto my
body, as dust stirred with
dust and enslaved my blood,
when will the hour come again,
the avalanche tumbling down?
When will the hour come?
I'm the honey of a gurgling star,
I come apart.
As tiger and conqueror I ruined
everything.
Law,
the passion to destroy one's own seal,
how should I do it if you
won't make love?
How, if you won't even put your
hands on my shoulder?
Kiss me, peony, touch me
as in time past.
Don't, don't be a loser,
don't loiter in my paintings
yellow pungent plant, the only one
which can calm a volcano,
the heaviest, softest hand,
which to crush myself
I created.

FOU DE VINCENT

I

The names that the sun gives itself are not enough. It is not
over yet. We are still sweet, fragile, dead. The palm that goes
to the throat of the beak, sideways, like a sword, can remain
lying there. As a drop of sweat can strike you on the forehead.
What was Dr. Gachet doing those forty hours on the fields
that later became the property of Smilja's mother-in-law?
Was he changing his sheets? Was he watching the dripping?
But what can we do, were the last words to Theo. You are
not the simple reseller of Corot. You are consecrated.
You take part in the battle. The too strong light starts
to exert pressure. The birds hurt like black bubbles. The tongue
shakes, it rolls like a wounded whale. The form disturbs
him, it is too big. The skin crushes daisies. It lies across
the brook and the little mills. Surrenders beneath your feet.

II

There are white ones and black ones. The crows
do not fly above water but above fields. The seagulls
wipe the hills. To them, the memory of blueness,
they are a sandwich in a trap, it is enough that they can
fly to Mostar. I watched them, too. When I shared in
the girls. Then I could still distribute people. Is friction
between living and dead resellers of canvases real?
The paintings are dressed. The man, a scroll
in him, smolders like a cigar. The bell announces
the lifting of barriers. The dry docks fill up. The matter,
you will hold out. Beneath morass, beneath hot
iron. You ignite the mass of water. Who knocks
when the sky lacerates? Shards are only the shards
of emptiness. You jump on them like a ballet dancer,
with a spare bunch of flowers. The skin is to be eaten.
We are the bag. We are the big black fiery pork fat that
pinches and pinches until you touch silk and glue
with your tongue and you recognize the traveler.

AGAIN THE ROADS ARE SILENT

again the roads are silent, dark peace
again there are bees, honey, silent green fields
willows by the rivers, stones at the bottom of the valleys
hills in the eyes, sleep in the animals

again the children are restless, blood in the whistles
again there is bronze in the bells, an aura in the tongue
travelers greet one another, the plague strengthened the joints
wild deer are in the palm, the snow shines

I see the morning, how I hurry
I see skin in the pious dust
I see shrieks of joy, how we head toward the south
Toledo man, two little hitchhikers

the images are clear, the flowers are timid
dark sealed sky, I hear a scream
the time for love awaits, time of tall statues
silent clear hinds, dreamy linden trees

PUBLICATION ACKNOWLEDGMENTS

Grateful acknowledgment is made to the following publications, in which these poems first appeared.

Agni: "At Night Rabbits," "in winter"; *The American Poetry Review:* "Greek Island," "Robi," "Sonnet of a Slovenian," "The Whole of Life"; *Black Warrior:* "again the roads are silent"; *Chicago Review:* "Watching all these"; *Colorado Review:* "The Flashlight," "We Club Stars"; *Conduit:* "Buffalo"; *Crowd:* "Children's Froth, Children's Clothing"; *Electronic Poetry Review:* "Incredulous Grandson"; *Exquisite Corpse:* "Look, Brother"; *Fence:* "The Letter"; *Fulcrum:* "Firmament Above the Cathedral"; *Hunger Mountain:* "Jumping on the Cart Full of Cantaloupes"; *The Iowa Review:* "To Immerse the Weight," "Ridges of aromatic"; *Maisonneuve:* "Home"; *The New Republic:* "Where Are You"; *The Ninth Letter:* "Kashogi," "Poem for Cindy Kleine," "Central Park," "The Circle and the Circle's Argument," "The Breeding of Prince"; *Pretext:* "To Metka," "Snow Is All That's Left"; *Prague Literary Review:* "Nile," "his favorite ride"; *Red Hydra Press* (chapbook): "again the roads are silent"; *The Rialto:* "The Writing"; *Six by Six:* "Good Morning," "Ballad for Metka Krašovec"; *Skein:* "The Flashlight," "Questions for Little Frogs"; *Third Bed:* "Coming Back," "Day"; *Third Coast:* "the lime in the desert," "Little Fears," "Fou de Vincent"; *Three Lands, Three Generations:* "Good Morning," "Borromini"; *Dragonfire:* "To the Heart"; *Gulf Coast:* "Young Creatures"; *Orient Express:* "Young Creatures"; *Poetry Review* (London): "The Apple."

"To Have a Friend," "To the Heart," "threw myself on the lid," "The Writing," "Dog," "Ring the Bell," "To Metka," "Greek Island," "in winter," "Fou de Vincent," and "again the roads are silent" also appeared in the chapbook *The Writing*, Contemporary World Poetry, AARK Arts, London, 2004.

INDEX OF POEMS AND TRANSLATORS

1962–1995—*poet and Joshua Beckman*

again the roads are silent—*poet and Christopher Merrill*

Apple, The—*poet and Anselm Hollo*

At Night Rabbits—*Ana Jelnikar and Peter Richards*

Ballad for Metka Krašovec—*poet and Joshua Beckman*

Borromini—*Andrew Wachtel*

Breeding of Prince, The—*poet and Peter Richards*

Buffalo—*poet and Joshua Beckman*

Central Park—*poet and Peter Richards*

Cetinje—*Ana Jelnikar and Christopher Merrill*

Children's Froth, Children's Clothing—*poet and Christopher Merrill*

Circle and the Circle's Argument, The—*Ana Jelnikar and Peter Richards*

Coming Back—*poet and Joshua Beckman*

Day—*poet and Anselm Hollo*

Dog—*Ana Jelnikar and Peter Richards*

Firmament Above the Cathedral—*poet and Peter Richards*

Flashlight, The—*poet and Peter Richards*

Fou de Vincent—*poet and Joshua Beckman*

Good Morning—*Andrew Wachtel*

Greek Island—*poet and Christopher Merrill*

his favorite ride—*poet and Anselm Hollo*

History Always Exploits Only Steam—*poet and Joshua Beckman*

Home—*Ana Jelnikar and Peter Richards*

Incredulous Grandson—*poet and Matthew Rohrer*

in winter—*poet and Elliott Anderson*

It Is Too Hot—*poet and Joshua Beckman*

(it's you)—*poet and Christopher Merrill*

Jumping on the Cart Full of Cantaloupes—*poet and Peter Richards*

Kashogi—*poet and Peter Richards*
Letter, The—*poet and Matthew Rohrer*
lime in the desert, the—*poet and Anselm Hollo*
Little Fears—*poet and Joshua Beckman*
Look, Brother—*poet and Anselm Hollo*
Nile—*poet and Elliott Anderson*
(Not the murder)—*poet and Matthew Rohrer*
(One day)—*poet and Anselm Hollo*
Poem for Cindy Kleine—*poet and Peter Richards*
Porcini—*poet and Joshua Beckman*
Questions for Little Frogs—*poet and Peter Richards*
Ridges of aromatic—*Ana Jelnikar and Peter Richards*
Ring the Bell—*poet and Joshua Beckman*
Robi—*Ana Jelnikar and Christopher Merrill*
Sheets and Embalming—*poet and Christopher Merrill*
Snow Is All That's Left—*Ana Jelnikar and Peter Richards*
Sonnet of a Slovenian—*Marko Jakše and Christopher Merrill*
Talk with the Hairdresser from Tashkent, The—*poet and Joshua
    Beckman*
threw myself on the lid—*poet and Anselm Hollo*
To Have a Friend—*poet and Anselm Hollo*
To Immerse the Weight—*poet and Christopher Merrill*
To Metka—*Ana Jelnikar and Christopher Merrill*
To the Heart—*poet and Christopher Merrill*
(Watching all these)—*poet and Matthew Rohrer*
We Club Stars—*Ana Jelnikar and Peter Richards*
Where Are You—*poet and Anselm Hollo*
Whole of Life, The—*poet and Christopher Merrill*
Writing, The—*poet and Phillis Levin*
Volga—*poet and Joshua Beckman*
Young Cops—*poet and Phillis Levin*
Young Creatures—*poet and Christopher Merrill*